Mirro

m a r i n a

or Me

b l i t s h t e y n

Fonograf Editions
Edited by Adie B. Steckel, Ellena Basada & Jeff Alessandrelli
Portland, OR & New York City, NY

Cover and text design by Mike Corrao

First Edition, First Printing
BUNNY08

Published by BUNNY, c/o Fonograf Editions
www.bunnypresse.org
www.fonografeditions.com

Distributed by NYU Press
NYUPress.org

The manufacturer's authorized representative in the EU for product safety is Mare Nostrum Group B.V., Mauritskade 21D, 1091 GC Amsterdam, The Netherlands. Email: gpsr@mare-nostrum.co.uk.

[clmp]
Fonograf Editions is a proud member of the Community of Literary Magazines and Presses

ISBN: 978-1-964499-60-4
ISBN (ebook): 978-1-964499-61-1

'your luck' and 'softest core' were published in *Thayer* Issue 2, in September 2024, selected by Erin White

MIRROR ME

MARINA BLITSHTEYN

BUNNY

i.

object lesson

mirror me, i say
hot for home
make an oval
there
push some breath through
you'll feel flutters
on your upper lip
a butterfly wing
a labia
to say true
in accentia
you need force
follow me
you need fear
a whirlwind
chasing you
you need bars
echo chambers
a cave of a mouth
where i live no
ghosts roam
because it's all ghosts
all walls for heroes
to try their tongues on
and my name too
a complex
you want all rounds
all the time blues

one big ache
to put your first through
but i say curl
your fingers first
i say turn around
roll your ares
say it to me again
you're close
you're very close

wake up typing with your right hand
leaning on your left
later than desire lets on
waiting for milky way memories
i think fondly of other planets
orbiting my new old look
i remember the dawns there
in each bed on each surface
venus is always thin above me
on mars i've felt my cheeks burn
no one tells you about saturn
i take the slide dreaming of snow
i'm hot but can't feel the wind
i'm colder now and the air is wet
i'm never satisfied in the morning
i crowd my pillow with them

your luck

he walked in gallantly like   a soul on two stilts
i told him i wasn't scared anymore   he said false
he said try your luck   elsewhere or else
you'll suffer forever   he said on his stilt legs
i can balance your mother   for you if you want
i met his folks   nothing but commonplaces
missteps all around   pleases and thank yous
i spilled butter   on my blouse but found a way out
let it slip that i'm lonely   lost myself to his advances
that i believed in romance once and now   it spells
doom in me   domestic goddesses   goblins robbing
me blind   heaven help the heavenless around a slim
oddly handsome gentleman   what he'll tell you no
master of mischief could promise you   what he does
is rescue you from your better self   in exchange for
pleasantries and fantasies   what he does is clever
and casual   a calisthenics for your feminisms
he barely walked out like a man   just airs and doubts
of a past life   steam and dust for a lost future scene
he said   to remember you by   and took off cool
his legs knocking on the floor like a dead doorknob

clair de lune

the superior way you hold yourself
pretend it isn't raining

the way you've trained yourself
to look surprised at the sky

every night a new place for you
every night demanding its own atlas

the house you've built for yourself
the way you hide yourself there

of all the other moons you loom
thread and spindle

of all the other moons you mound
crack and cradle

the way you list among the bodies
as the wistful one

how you mourn yourself by day
but stay a ghost

a loose dress

my heart hangs heavy here
with everyone i've ever loved
i wore a wrap dress hung
like a hug, i wore a strapless
little number that lagged
like a useless embrace
i've affixed their names
each one to a hem
first there were many
and they all wanted airs
then it got colder out
so i huddled up to a navy
blue turtleneck made of wool
then i got used to the heat
around my neck like hands
so i found one who made
me call him every day
i wanted it to fit tight
i wanted to feel tense in it
now i can appreciate
a lighter cotton frock
from my mother's era
now it's summer again
and i want to wear black
but this linen is lighter

self-portrait

with my big hand over my little hand

with flat glass covering my face

with a mustache no man wants to see

with tire marks already lining it

with a big old boot print smearing it

with two blank looks to my name

with a dangling modifier to account for

with only one proposition for you

cherry picking

tonight you're marrow-mouthed
set like the seediest cell
from which a well springs
plum and all
i wish you well

yesterday you fed yourself twice
once out of habit and then
you handed yourself to the desert
nothing could quell that will
no blood broke through

who knows what fortune
folds out before you tomorrow
stick to your kettles
your lackluster kites
barely an air quote
a barrel with no falls flat

for now you choke-hold
whatever opens its heart to you
milk it for its aura
purple like eggplants purple
like pear bruises
like black cherry juice

petrichor

you have to pay
attention i told
myself in the rain
this window has
earned that from
you you have to
sit and smell it
until you've
memorized how
this feels until
you recognize
everything after
as either instances
or offspring of
that rain you
have to imagine
there is a body
somewhere in
the world right
now that smells
like this rain and
then when you
meet it and
come close to
it you can feel
it on them this
impregnable
magical opening
this unimaginable

the self roams

the heart recedes

the horizon arches

the ceiling widens

the sense of self

the image of it

how fluid it is

how it moves

its maybe waves

its maladies

the right notes

a window now

having a sense

having a hint of it

k i n

dreamt i spun
myself into a blade
from nothing
told myself i came
from nothing and now
i glimmer like a god
dreamt i hollowed out
my ivory handle until
i was all shell all husk
until the silence inside
swirled into a roar
until the tempests spoke
in me and said you bone
you silver-footed root
you wisp of a woman
nothing crawls through you
and to nothing you'll crawl
on your shins like a snake
with no charmer like shards
of broken glass in the sand
but not ground small enough
to turn to sand, you made
a wonder of yourself and now
you sheen enough to count
you can't count on me
you can't count on us
we can't save you in this skin

d e s i r e

something sings
i believe it
anyone
brutal
sparks
hemlocks
hanging roots
something hands
loosely
empathy
entropy
charming
something blinks
53 54 55 56

d i s c 4

i'm in love with a man with the name of a whore,
not any whore but thee whore, the sophistication
of language gaged it--how can i abandon you,
a strong leader, a man with a plan, when you say
suck it it's clear, language is crystal, hold me down
so i get the meaning--how have i forsaken you
in exchange for american dollars--now i keep
a little emblem with me in my head, somewhere
in a keepsake box, some trinkets, lenin, stalin,
little gold pins--you're worth nothing to me now,
you're nothing but a dirty little whore to play with

d i s c   3

don't hide your grief from me, mother
country--everybody needs a dick in
the head--he said you suck a mean
dick and i thought that's the title for
something, anything, everything--
later i'm abandoning your intrigue,
how you hide your face from me,
the face of men, all lined up to kill,
like kill, like killers--i spent my life
avoiding men like you but they make
countries happen, money happen,
worlds go round--

d i s c   2

then later my lips too thin to wipe it clean
i knew i had to take it further--maybe the metaphor
has the feel of the universe expanding, in space
or in a woman's body--either way derrida meant
my body was the field, my body was the ground,
my body was the border within which countries
happen, die out then happen, make paper then
fold, then happen from ruins, from bodies, from
forms--i knew it like i knew the back of my own
hand, having stared at it in moments of sorrow--

d i s c 1

i knew it as the instrument and the only instrument,
my only currency but too young to handle it i kept
tabs on it in crayon boxes then later in pockets
then later in bags then later changed its nature
to the stature of plastic--nothing had the same feel
like that first real silver, that first real disk in my desk,
that time i slipped it around my fingers and put
my whole mouth over it--i knew it was my instrument,
my only instrument, the only piece of currency i'd need

it's me i fall in love with
me i carry
to the edge of myself
only to let go
over and over
and u wait there patiently
on the other end like a priest
like the river styx
with my form in ur hands
guiding me through it
come u say over
and over

ii.

in another tongue.
i said it's the only thing

that comes easy.

i said you know
what i mean.

coriander.
sycamore.
cilantro.

i said both havens
wouldn't want me.

you only
get one.

i said you wished
you could follow her.

a minister.
cicada.
a priest.

the only suffering
that mattered.

your door
to your wall.

a forearm up
from having to.

lilium.
lacquer.
clove.

you said you wasted
your breath.

i looked for you
in millions.

i told myself i know
i know and tried.

aplomb.
appellate.
maple.

god banished us
this hungry.

i said you hear
yourself. i call you

from another room
and sometimes here.

honeysuckle.
sorghum.
wheat.

effluvia.
banister.
fern.

when you were a martyr
you meant it.

when you were meringue.
when plums boiled

over sugar water.
when i tasted it warm.

when you administered
the syrup. when you

pinched vanilla.
when you stirred.

spatula.
simplex.
foal.

porcelain.
linden.
dill.

in the lake of frozen togethers

isn't it always too hot or too cold

can't we see ourselves waiting to be happy

can't we imagine a better end

when we wake up in the morning

can't we count on the negative feelings

can't we keep yelling for our moms

can't we try our surrender over

a possible kitchen, a possible couch

a sun room someone else could call a reading room

when we stop ourselves from crippling self doubt

aren't we already living the lives we intended

me: you can't abandon yourself

your life in marionettes
your sonnet booms
little lily aprons
gingham skirts
a marble rye
in your finest
a term exhaust
seven deadly faiths
what love demanded
a protagonistic eye
a dutiful daughter
staid diplomacy
for your parent types
everybody ever wanted
everybody dictates doom
the news
its citizens
language in loops
a purity in this
solutions
silhouettes of men
and body stumps
you dump them
under your bed
your monsters sweep
through your bedroom door
your mother on the phone
enter: solitude

enter: elliptical fears
enter: draped in death
you in your lost bed
you with your ghosts
a pine with eyes gets up
bends and scurries away
in the dream you're tonal
in love with the forest
matricide blues
living etymologies
borders evolve, blur
cause entropy in parts
some deeper etch of you
a constellation cannot tell
a step decided
little causes
little poor surrenders
you observe yourself
committing lies
you punt the lines
you persevere

it takes

a little
takes a little more
pull yourself
together
it's always
3 o'clock
in the afternoon
when your mom calls
upset about you
it's always a real
dark night
in your mind
when you dream
about death and
flying
a little of
both
it pulls
a little
after you
your friend says
you lean in that
direction
which direction
is that
you ask her
she says
without answering

notes for the head of a queen

the crown goes
to you
cut her off
at the root
if it sizzles
it's splitting
if it spits
that's it
whose neck
was fit
for a queen
the better
to doom
you with
my dear
whose chin
sticks out
like a spire
your highness
your highness

men
bound in
with gifts
at their wrists
ladies in
hats
bat lashes

for lashes
bust to
bust
men brave
moats of
fur and
hair for this
drop crumbs
on old shoulders
joking your
highness your
highness

she was mum
once too
wept blue
sapphire
tears
ate every
one
then food
ran out
then cake
then mum
said get
the hell out
they come
for your
head first
your
highness

who loves
the moon
a pearl
in the mouth
who eyes it
half full
of light
the rest
in death
who begs
for moon
like dogs
howling
hungrier
than a lion
your highness
loves it
your highness

softest core

take turns
  at the heart

first plunge the fabric
  dye-stricken tricked out

first locate
the heart crane your neck

  first dislodge
yourself from your self

at base the breath
follows slick-handed

slack-jawed honey

  lapis lily white
pre-syncope

  then tell your oracle

try a myriad try telepath
  try main

take your artery
your artillery out

  a shock of odds
then nada

what we offer

make bread   make wine   make holidays

wrapping paper for your gifts
elevated sense of import

ultimately you matter   so much to the world

waste your time   on bread dipped   in butter

apologize   confess   contain yourself
nobody means to take your gifts away

you were born with nothing   leave with less

we can make you feel   in love along the way

the key

there is the butcher
there is the key
to the shop
there's meat
off a beam
just hanging

who among us
can name the way
these bodies hang

not the butcher
not his buyers
and there is no key

notes to self

set news aside

feed the magicians

bring a sweater

in another 20 mins

communities turn on u

illusion of work

steal the post-its

send package tmrw

pack an umbrella

read more about marxism

criticism is not the end

check bad habits

mind ur needs

the apple

every day you complain your tree roots backwards
sinks its limbs into sky like new teeth
clutches you where your heart is new
you can't let go of the hurt
                                        you felt in the pit
where new seeds burst in pairs
counting on you to balance
every day you lament your thinness of skin
resent the leaves for elevating
and you think if this were heaven you would fall
                                        already with the darker things
you think if this were hell you would be free of it

this is the wall

at my house we surf the news breaking

scan the wreckage for survivors
if we've known any faces
we'll see them again

this time with our palms pressed to our mouths

*

don't go, they said
and then they said, leave prayers for us

*

i'm telling you the bells
break me

at jesus' tomb all women
covered their heads

dusted the stone with handkerchiefs
they brought to their lips

if i was ever thirsty it'd be there

but i got too dizzy in the desert
and i was promised a brook

i shuffled around like an american
in love with your ruins

*

this is the wall she said
gesturing

a toy gun found its way out a car window in front of us

is this a joke i asked
gesturing

*

toy guns and toy soldiers line the wall
red ribbons and strings for our sins
a flock of disconsolate beggars

i drop another woman's prayer on the ground where no
    one will hear it
if this is worth a damn i might as well turn my back to it
    all when i go

*

looks like i escaped with all my heads in my hands
at least 3 warring visions of the same flag
i chew my fingers up about it now

i'm trying to peel the prints off so i can travel
safely from place to place across all borders
one layer of skin means i'm an american

two means i'm home and three means
i'm free

the loot in your lot

a metaphor for speaking
                                                  having spoken

welcome to you and you

only the posies are mine
only the way i bind them are mine

dangle off the root in your rot

you warble it, marble it, mumble

                              subtracting a negative thing

or have i been everything, every one

making believe

daughter

i've met someone who's not myself
i left a body by the kitchen, age 5

handing over her neck for slaughter

isn't it rare to be such a dutiful daughter
and still ask for nothing in return

haven't i earned the chance to perish

some day i'll cherish the memories
clock on the stove will stall and stall

but i'll be along for it all, the strangle,
the murder, the hiding of knives, age 5

isn't it rare to announce your passing

i'm lashing out at myself, before i go
you'll know the shape of it

by 15 the body was gone but the space of it
loomed in the room, i recognize the lurk

from years of therapy, i've met a man

who wasn't him and some who were
i buried all of them but they roam

mother forgive me my indolence
remember you want this for me

to be free of your memories too

isn't it rare to want all of it, even the chokes
even the stomach that lodged in your throat

i was the kind to spare none of it
i was ahead at the front of it, age 5

i watched and watched you suffer it

i'm offering you a way out, you say
with yourself in tow, i want that for you

who martyrs the madder marauders
who mirrors the iron in stoves

i've met a new man and i'm over it

being in love with my past, my post
my purple openings, stall and stole

the head for the hole, the crow
for the crown, i fold for all of it

go caw around somebody else's business
show me forgiveness, forgiveness

the look to shock

embrace unoriginal
propose a walk with yourself

score points in practice

propose a theory of daily life

really an embarrassment of riches
really a richness to you

so much to be grateful for

you forget to hide it from others

i had to refer to myself

it landed as
allusion to the sound
i said she or her
and meant multiples
meant myriads
meant miriam and mira
and all other names
all other fractures
upon meeting new
people all others

i had to count myself
among them for fear
of being an island
but there is no self
without them isn't
that so dear reader
there is no you
without me here

Land

m a r i n a

guage

b l i t s h e y n

Fonograf Editions
Edited by Adie B. Steckel, Ellena Basada & Jeff Alessandrelli
Portland, OR & New York City, NY

Cover and text design by Mike Corrao

First Edition, First Printing
BUNNY08

Published by BUNNY, c/o Fonograf Editions
www.bunnypresse.org
www.fonografeditions.com

Distributed by NYU Press
NYUPress.org

The manufacturer's authorized representative in the EU for product safety is Mare Nostrum Group B.V., Mauritskade 21D, 1091 GC Amsterdam, The Netherlands. Email: gpsr@mare-nostrum.co.uk.

[clmp]

Fonograf Editions is a proud member of the Community of Literary Magazines and Presses

ISBN: 978-1-964499-60-4
ISBN (ebook): 978-1-964499-61-1

sonnet: mutter and sonnet: eyn were previously published in *Hyperallergic* on April 3, 2019 by Wendy Xu

LANDGUAGE

Marina Blitshteyn

BUNNY

Contents

s o n n e t : m u t t e r

bitte, this city, better to see you
with, better for seething, bitte, and please
remember it pleasing, betting on you
and won, my city, my gott, and stippled
with sun splattered leaves, better to leave you
seeming to love me, better to seek you
out of the rubble of my leben, love,
bitte, liebe, i left my mutter, mum,
her mother, her name was libbe, i moved
to citty, to set my grieving aside,
and bitte, behold, unbidden, i left
its light in my heart, good riddance citte
my citte a citte bitte unlit
like a match spit on, unsmitten, unmet
after all, unfall, unbitten apple

a city

at the mouth of hoyt lake where a boy once
told me he loved me, where a boy once said
he loved another woman, where a boy
said happy 1 year anniversary,
where I picked a wild flower as a kid
and it grew for a week without water,
where I played badminton with my cousin,
where I could see a big grand piano
when the night was black and the lights were long
along the surface, I took myself there
in early fall to marvel at the trees
and wonder if it's always looked like this.

homes

Once you see something you can't unsee it--

How anxious my mother is, how angry,

how loud my sister is on the phone, dad's

bad habit, how green this city is, or

can be, this corner where a kid was killed,

this block where Todd lived, where we worked before

what happened, and Elmwood, my beloved,

where I took my friends, how white we are here,

and why is that, how 2 blocks over homes

are in foreclosure while we're in cafes.

palaces

oh the palaces you'll go, the glass walls
cold but welcoming, old metropolis
new metropolis, doors whose names you'll learn
to pronounce, titles with surnames, proper
prophecies, with property to their names,
puppetry of luxury and order.
at your laxest you unlace your mother
from yourself, her same chip on your shoulder,
you can undemand americanness
from your name. at your worst you hoist your flag
of unbelonging with extravagance,
a vagrancy of birth, your father's shame.

questions

whose city is this   is the same question
as whose story is this to tell. cities
constructed on stories,   sand over sand.
isaac and I had been a city, matt
and I were a city, now in ruins.
                     are some stories not mine to tell if I
live in them, if I bear witness? cities
constructed on ethics,   sand over sand.
our contract as citizens not to just
burn the libraries, flood the museums.

questions

So where are you from. Where is your name from.
How long have you been here. What languages
do you speak. What languages do you speak
at home. What languages do your parents
speak. How funny. Have you ever been back.
Have you wanted to. Do you like it here.
So where is home for you. Where is home for
your name. Do you still have family there.
Do you visit them often. How nice. How
long does it take. Do you like it so far.

the return

I can’t say it, we would never say it,
cheesy-now? no, Кишинёв, Молдова,
not *Kiszyniów* or even Кишинів,
not Кишинэу to us, no, קעשענעוו,
פאגראם קעשענעוו, City of Slaughter,
city of my parents’ youth, where they chant
old street names over and over in cabs,
complaining about the new currency—
what was it like back then, I’m asking them
over and over, the way a mourner
turns and returns to the loss asking why.

g o o d s

who gave you the right? well no one, i got it
from you. and what makes you think? i don't mean
to offend you. where did you learn all this?
i was raised in this city, i lay claims
to this city, i pay tribute to this
city. these aren't your names to say. how old
were you when you came? we were refugees
to this city, you gave us donations,
we went to goodwill to sift through your goods.
don't throw anything out, i learned, one man's
trash is another woman's history.

tourism

I love it here, he said on the boardwalk
looking out over Coney Island Beach.
It was barely spring and mostly empty
save for a few grey seagulls wandering
under a cold grey sky. He brought us here
off-season to see, we all took the train
for hours just to have hot dogs and pose
in front of the boarded-up skating rink.
I love it here, he told me and only
me and nobody in particular.
Everything's trash, the beach is trash, the sand
is trash, the people are trash, I love it.

Russian

Later we wandered into a Russian
restaurant where I spoke Russian and smoked.
We ordered vodka bottles at unfixed
prices, it started to rain, I felt least
qualified to speak for all of us and
least at home among the smoked meats, among
my Russian airs, with these Americans.
You can't smoke in here, our waitress told me
and only me and everyone with me
in formal Russian, meaning you plural.

American

Since then I learned just be American,
speak American, act American
and they'll treat you better. Then when I lived
near Brighton Beach I pretended not to
know Russian, speak Russian, act as Russian
but they smelled the Russian on me. I was
among my kind for the first time but walked
around like I was better than that, like
I was over it, like I escaped and
now I was found, I was American.

free

What would it take to feel free? My student
said love the prison. Sarah said that facts
can be a productive limitation,
she means like a formal constraint, like verse.

Tonight I check my bank account and cope
the only way I know how—I build more
rows of these, more and more cells in the room
so I can practice dancing in tight spaces.

i s

ignorance is bills—wait—so if knowledge
is power then ignorance is weakness—
wait—if ignorance is bliss then knowledge
is sadness—wait—power equals money,
money equals power—hold up—minute
after minute, hour after hour—
wait—if time is money there's no such thing
as a free lunch—wait—knowledge is power
is sadness is free—ignorance is bills

interlude

the goal posts move, the rules change up on you,
that's what it's like to make it, you look up
how to eat with silverware on your phone,
you're googling what's a good wine to order,
you're making mistakes in conversations
with your friends, your friends went on vacations
to islands you've never heard of, you keep
a list in your head, liquors, good cheeses,
what's served with which and how you should like it,
but later, this is just an interlude.

class

You're so Buffalo, he said, and meaning
to wound me, meaning I'm not passing for
Manhattan, meaning my little habits
or mannerisms aren't matching, meaning
they're giving me away, they're keeping me
where I'm from, I'm acting like where I'm at
not where I'm going, like I just don't know
and my Buffalo is showing, like I
haven't been here long enough, and even
if I had I wouldn't even own it.

poetrying

It's a bit like Olson in a corset.
Or like Julie Carr said, 'I, Minimus.'

A subjectivity, apology.
The opposite of objectivism.

The apposite. A position paper
on gender, gender performance, bondage.

A one-woman show. Like Maggie Nelson,
propositions. Or full-on proposals.

A burlesque of citizenship, friendship,
appropriation. A shame exercise.

Apropos of poverty, poetry,
pottery, port authority, trying.

m o o d r i n g s

be reasonable, be personable,
lover of full disclosure, be fulfilled
in your dayjob, your nightjob, your seasons
timed to your trysts, be true to your moodrings,
selfish and fraught as they are, they tie you
home to your transience, your wayward escapes,
they teach you adaptive habits, your name
ending in flexible vowels, even
your apathy, like it doesn't matter,
not names, not languages, not who you are.

you can't show this to anyone, only
strangers. change your name or something. no one
has to know. it doesn't have to be you.
it doesn't have to mean anything. it's
not necessarily yours. you can't tell
anyone. just keep my name out of it.
keep your friends. you can't show your hand like that.
you can't bite the hand that feeds you. trust me.
keep your enemies closer. what's the worst
that could happen. so no one knows your name.

weather

weather is a social fabric, a thread,
it kinda has to be, or else we all
fall down, or else the bridge is falling down,
or else they build more walls, or else the dam
breaks, and the levies, or else the waters
swallow us, or else the center cannot
hold, or else the circuits crumble, or else
the grids collapse, the network fails us, or
else, or else the shores erode, or ruins,
or we shore against them, or we rage, rage
against the dying, ring around them, ashes.

there's a rot in your heart. don't turn away.
there's a rock in your softest part. listen.
it's growing with you. an eye for an eye.
there's an eye in your hand sometimes. some day
you'll be able to see it. don't look down.
you'll be able to see yourself clearer.
there's a cloud in your sky sometimes. someone
will see who you are. someone will show you.
someone will hold you to you. who is it.
who is that somebody. who can you know.
is it you. is it you. is it you.

russian poet

here it is then, мама мая, take it
away from me, just get it out of me,
боже мой, что тут такое special,
можно подумать, it's just a little
word or two, whatever, no one will know
how bad you speak it, молчи, better to
remain silent and be thought a fool right,
дура ты, you want everyone to see,
уйди, уходи от сюда, кто ты
такая, тоже мне, russian poet.

you hear differently when I'm talking to
you. I talk differently too. stories
sound more interesting than a narrative.
the truth is I'm not one for arc. I can't
control myself. the punchlines more punchy
than nuanced. the limits presupposing
an end. an end presupposing climax.
but the climb is nonlinear, rhythmic,
punctuated by doubt. coming to terms
then over them. like jacques derrida's step
beyond. or walter benjamin's threshold
experience. or worse, like graham greene's last
words: oh why does it take so long to come?

mishmash

it's coming together now, все вместе,
like my people say (which people?) like my
favorite band says, everything in its
right place (english) or like my country is
(the only one) a melting pot of tongues,
of moods, blood sausages of languages
i pick up like scraps for a dog (a bitch)
i chew on like bones (кости) i suck on
like my own teeth (ציינדעלע) like i cut
my teeth on this mishmash momeloshen

landguage

Still you can feel alienated from
your own language, like it's still an English
they're speaking and not (which version?) even
if you're a native speaker (how native?)
even if you're from around here (like where?)—
I'm on a bus riding through The Village
of Lisle and can't read its graffiti, or
I'm at a conference on Poetry and
Political Theory and can't access
a talk. Still a stranger in a strange lag.

s o n n e t : e y n

i've already staked my fate to my name
like a fool in dual languages, dura,
дура, like a duel in foul languages,
сука, a bitch, the first thing they teach you
door in four languages, all of them closed
drool in foal languages, all of then nay
dour in fuel languages, all of them lit
droll in full languages, all of them laid
the first thing they teach you, блядь, like a whore
blyat, like a splatter, blat, like a bullet,
blit, like a little, shteyn, like a lot, stain,
like it matters, stone, as in not, then n.

BUNNY

OTHER BUNNY TITLES

1. **Warren Longmire—***BIRD/DIZ [an erased history of bebop]* (print)

2. **Bill Carty—***We Sailed on the Lake* (print)

3. **Zoe Tuck—***Bedroom Vowel* (print)

4. **Michael Wheaton—***Home Movies* (print)

5. **Jennifer Quartararo—***An Aribtrary Formation of Unspecified Value* (print)

6. **Matthew Broaddus—***Deeper the Tropics* (print)

7. **Katie Naughton—***Debt Ritual* (print)

Inspired by the work of the multitudinous artist Ray Johnson, BUNNY is an imprint of Fonograf Editions. Publishing a wide variety of works, BUNNY is looking towards the future while thinking about the past.